SCARY SCIENCE

24 Creepy Experiments

Shar Levine and Leslie Johnstone

Illustrations by Ashley Spires

■ SCHOLASTIC

New York Toronto London Auckland
Sydney Mexico City New Delhi Hong Kong

ISBN 978-0-545-32406-9

10 9 8 7 6 5 4 3 2 1   11 12 13 14 15

Printed in the U.S.A. 40
First American edition, August 2011

TABLE OF CONTENTS

INTRODUCTION

Are you the kind of person who enjoys a good scare? If you are, then this is the book for you. But if you're more timid, there's nothing to fear. You are about to scare others silly.

This book won't teach you how to become a witch or a wizard. It won't turn you into a ghost, ghoul, or goblin, but it will help you amaze your friends and wow your parents. Now, don't tell a soul (living or dead), but you won't be using any magic or conjuring up creatures; you will be using science to perform some very remarkable spooky feats.

Along the way you will also learn cool facts about real-life werewolves, zombies, vampires, and other things that may make you leave the light on at night.

DISCLAIMER

Are ghosts, goblins, zombies, wicked witches, wizards, or ghouls real? The authors have never seen any of these things, have never cast spells, and don't believe in them. But they do believe in science as an explanation. The activities in this book are meant to be educational and to help you understand how science is part of your everyday life. When confronted with strange or unexplained phenomena, look for an answer in science first!

WARNING TO YOUNG SCIENTISTS

There is very little that can hurt a ghost, but there are many things that can hurt *you*. Make sure you follow all the steps in the experiments exactly as they are written. If you aren't sure if something is all right to do, ask an adult.

Dos

1. Make sure an adult is with you while you do the experiments.
2. Immediately tell an adult if you or someone else is hurt in any way.
3. Have an adult go over all the steps of the experiment with you, and have an adult give you all the materials you need to perform the activity.
4. Tie back long hair, and roll up your sleeves.
5. Help clean up after each activity, and wash your hands before and after touching any food or drink.
6. Ask an adult to throw away the materials you've used to make the concoctions.

Don'ts

1. Do not eat, drink, or taste any of the experiments unless the instructions say you can.
2. Do not do an experiment if you are allergic to any of the ingredients in it. Tell an adult about any allergies before doing these activities.
3. Do not feed any experiments to other people or to animals.
4. Do not gather your own materials without supervision or substitute any ingredients for the ones listed in the book.
5. Do not change the instructions or recipes in the book.
6. Do not handle sharp objects or use any equipment that plugs into a wall.

NOTE TO PARENTS AND TEACHERS

This book is designed to help young children discover some basic scientific principles. We recommend adult supervision, as children may not always read the instructions. Make sure you go over all the steps with your children, so they know how to do the experiment. It's important to tell your budding scientists that raiding the kitchen cabinet for supplies may not be an acceptable thing to do. Children may also be fascinated with appliances and tools, so it is critical that you keep a close eye on your sorcerer's apprentices.

Unless specified in the instructions, children must not eat, drink, or taste the experiment or allow anyone else to do so, including the family pet.

1. SHRUNKEN HEADS

There really *is* such a thing as a shrunken head. The Jivaro tribesmen of South America were famed for taking the heads of their enemies, removing the skulls, and shrinking each one to about the size of an orange. This was called *tsantsa*. Here's a better way of making your own shrunken heads — without harming anyone.

You Will Need:
- an adult helper
- a large apple
- an apple peeler
- plastic carving tools: a grapefruit spoon (spoon with a serrated tip), a plastic knife, or the kind of plastic tool that comes with children's art supplies
- 4 cups (1 L) cold water
- a large mixing bowl
- 1 cup (250 mL) salt
- a spoon
- a wire rack
- a paintbrush
- shellac or varnish
- decorations: paint, glue, beads, feathers, yarn, etc.

What to Do
1. Have an adult peel the skin from the apple.
2. Using your carving tools, carve a face in the apple.
3. Pour cold water into the large mixing bowl and add in the salt. Use the spoon to stir until the salt dissolves.
4. Carefully drop the apple into the bowl of salty water, and leave it on a counter or table for a day.
5. Take the apple out and put it on a wire rack to dry. Leave it in a warm place for several weeks.
6. When the apple is dry, brush on a coat of shellac or varnish to seal it.

7. Now the fun part: Decorate the apple. You can paint the face with glow-in-the-dark paint, glue on scary beaded eyes, and stick on fur, feathers, straw, string, and hair.

BOO! WHAT HAPPENED?

The apple shrank and became wrinkled. Apples contain water, sugar, and salt. They can be dried and kept from spoiling by adding more salt. The extra salt in the water drew out the water in the apple. This movement of water from an area of less salt (the apple) to an area of more salt (the salty water) is called **osmosis**. Once the amount of salt was the same in both the water and the apple, the water stopped moving out. After you removed the apple from the mixture and placed it on a rack to dry, the salt was left behind, preserving the apple.

2. SPIDERWEBS

Have you ever done the "spider dance"? This is what happens when you walk into a spider's web and you get the sticky stuff all over your head, face, and clothing. Your arms flail through the air as you try to peel off the elastic strings from your body. This next experiment won't have you doing the shimmy in your kitchen.

You Will Need:
- an adult helper
- a tea bag (black tea, not green tea or herbal tea)
- a heatproof glass jar or cup
- hot water
- a spoon
- a fresh egg
- a coffee filter

What to Do
1. Place the tea bag into the glass jar or cup. Have an adult add very hot tap water to the container.
2. Use the spoon to stir the water, and allow the tea bag to sit in the cup for about an hour.
3. Have the adult separate the egg white from the yolk. Throw away the yolk. Take the tea bag out of the cup and add the egg white to the tea. Let the mixture sit for about four or five hours. Do not stir.

4. Strain the mixture through the coffee filter and remove the egg strands with your hands. What do they feel like? Allow the strands to dry, then feel them again. (Be sure to wash your hands after touching the egg strands.)

STRANGE! WHAT HAPPENED?

The egg white formed strands that look like the fibers of a spiderweb. Egg white is made of a type of **protein** called **albumin**. When chemicals in the tea, called **polyphenols**, came in contact with the egg white, they caused the protein strands to thicken. The strands of thicker protein were strong enough for you to remove from the egg and tea mixture.

STRANGE . . . BUT TRUE!

Most spiders aren't deadly, although bites from certain kinds might hurt a bit. If you live in Australia, you have to be very careful not to come into contact with the Sydney funnel-web spider, or *Atrax robustus*. It has huge fangs that can pierce through your clothing and even chomp into your finger- or toenails. If left untreated, a bite from this spider can kill a person in less than 15 minutes. Fortunately there is antivenom, a special injection that people can be given if they have been bitten.

3. HOWLING SPIRITS

There's an eerie sound coming from the graveyard. The sound is getting closer and closer. What *is* that horrible screech?

You Will Need:

- a large plastic cup
- a small pin
- a piece of thin string or dental floss about 2 feet (60 cm) long
- a toothpick

What to Do

1. Use the pin to poke a hole in the middle of the bottom of the plastic cup.
2. Thread the end of the string or dental floss through the cup so the long end of the string hangs outside of the top of the cup.
3. Tie the end of the string that is sticking out of the bottom of the cup around a toothpick. The toothpick will sit flat against the bottom of the cup and will keep the string from pulling through the hole.
4. Hold the cup in one hand and wet the fingers on your other hand. Pinch the string just inside the cup and slide your fingers down to the end of the string. Try pulling your fingers at different speeds and see how it changes the sound coming from the cup.

EEK! WHAT HAPPENED?

The exact sound you made depends on the string you used. The dental floss sounds like a creaky old wooden door being opened. If you play a guitar, you know that the sound of the instrument changes depending on how long or thick the string that you are strumming is: The longer or thicker the string, the lower the sound; the shorter or thinner the string, the higher the sound. The cup **amplified** the sound, or made the sound louder.

STRANGE . . . BUT TRUE!

The people in movies who create the special sound effects you hear are called foley artists, and they are named after Jack Foley, the man who pioneered this field. When you hear a sound and see an image, you naturally think that the two were made together. But in movies, that's not always the case. The sound of someone walking on fresh snow may be created by crushing cornflakes. Smashing a head of cabbage may sound like a zombie munching on a head. And letting the air out of an inflated balloon sounds like . . . well, try it and see!

4. FESTERING OOZE

Oozing green ooze pouring from the pores of an ogre might gross you out. Thick, yellow snot dripping from the wart on a witch's nose might make you gag. But this batch of goop will only make you laugh (although it could cause someone else to retch!).

You Will Need:

- an adult helper
- two small plastic or glass containers (empty baby food jars are perfect)
- ¾ cup (180 mL) white glue
- 2 drops glycerine (from a drug store)
- 2 drops yellow or green food coloring
- a wooden stir stick or a stick from a frozen treat
- 2 teaspoons (10 mL) borax (to be handled by an adult)
- ¼ cup (60 mL) water
- a sealable plastic bag or a plastic container with a lid

What to Do

1. Squirt the white glue, glycerine, and food coloring into a small plastic or glass container. Use the wooden stick to stir the mixture. Don't add too much glycerine, as the ooze will be too runny.
2. Have an adult place the borax into the other container with the water. Use the stir stick to mix this until most of the borax is dissolved.
3. Slowly pour the borax solution into the green or yellow goo. The mixture will begin to form strings. Continue adding the borax mixture and stirring until the ooze starts to hold together. You may not need all the borax mixture.
4. Pick up the ooze from the container and have fun turning yourself into a gross ooze monster. Do not put it in your eyes, nose, or any other open body part, like your ears or mouth, and make sure you don't have any cuts. Make sure you wash your hands after you have played with the ooze, and pour the remaining borax solution down the drain. You can store the ooze for up to three days in a sealable plastic bag or plastic container with a lid.

5. Do not flush the ooze or put it down the drain. Throw it in the garbage.

EEEW! WHAT HAPPENED?

White glue contains a material called polyvinyl alcohol, or PVA. This substance changes when it comes into contact with the borax solution. A chemical reaction takes place and the small individual particles, or **molecules**, of PVA join together. When these **polymers** (*poly* means "several" and *mer* comes from *merous*, which means "parts") come together, they make a slimy, bouncy ooze. By changing the amount of glycerine added to the glue, you can make an ooze that is more or less runny.

STRANGE . . . BUT TRUE!

Have you ever wondered why glue doesn't stick to the inside of the bottle? Glue is made up of several chemicals. One kind of chemical makes the glue sticky, and another makes it stay a liquid. When the glue is exposed to air outside the bottle, the chemical that keeps it liquid **evaporates**, or goes into the air. As this happens, the glue begins to stick. In the bottle there isn't much air on the surface of the glue, so not enough of the chemical can evaporate to cause the glue to harden.

5. FLESH-EATING ZOMBIE

In scary movies, zombies usually wear ripped, dirty clothes and have bits of rotting flesh dangling from them. Here's a simple way to temporarily look like a zombie.

You Will Need:

- an adult helper
- ½ cup (120 mL) cold water
- two small plastic or glass containers (empty baby food jars are perfect)
- 1 teaspoon (5 mL) guar gum (available in the baking section of health-food or specialty grocery stores)
- a wooden stir stick or a stick from a frozen treat
- 2 drops red food coloring
- ½ teaspoon (2.5 mL) borax (to be handled by an adult)
- 2 teaspoons (10 mL) hot tap water
- a sealable plastic bag

What to Do

1. Pour the cold water into one of the plastic or glass containers, then add the guar gum. Use the wooden stick to stir until the mixture is thick and cloudy.
2. Add the food coloring to the mixture and stir until it is blended in. Allow the container to stand for 5–10 minutes.
3. Have an adult add the borax to the second small container and pour in the very hot water. Use the stir stick to mix until the borax is dissolved.
4. Slowly pour the borax mixture into the container with the red guar gum liquid. Use the stir stick to swirl the liquids together. Then spread the new mixture out and turn yourself into a zombie! But don't put it in your eyes, nose, or any other open body part.
5. This gunk will keep for a few days in a sealed plastic bag. When you're done, throw the sealed bag in the garbage.

GROSS! WHAT HAPPENED?

This pink blobby gunk is — you guessed it! — another polymer. Guar gum is not like the pink, chewy stuff you use to blow bubbles. It's used as a thickener in foods. Guar gum comes from the guar plant, which grows in India and Pakistan. Guar gum is in many foods you eat, like ice cream and pudding. It's a natural polymer and binds with liquids to thicken them. It also keeps nasty ice crystals from forming in frozen foods.

6. DISAPPEARING COFFEE CUPS

In ghost stories, one way you know that there are spirits in the house is that things appear and disappear. We all know how to make fresh-baked cookies disappear (you eat them!), but coffee cups are a whole different matter.

You Will Need:
- an adult helper
- ⅓ cup (80 mL) nail polish remover with acetone
- a small glass bowl or metal container
- a Styrofoam cup
- a plastic knife or spoon
- Styrofoam packing chips

WARNING: This experiment must be performed in a well-ventilated area away from open flames, preferably outdoors. Have an adult supervise this activity. Do not eat or drink any of the liquids. Wash your hands after handling the materials.

What to Do
1. Pour the nail polish remover into the bowl.
2. Break the Styrofoam cup into pieces and place the pieces into the bowl. Watch what happens.
3. Have an adult use the plastic knife or spoon to remove the guck from the bottom of the bowl.
4. Repeat the experiment using the packing chips. Observe any difference in the amount of time they take to dissolve.

YEEPS! WHAT HAPPENED?

The acetone in the nail polish remover broke apart some of the connections between the **polystyrene** molecules of the Styrofoam cup. It did not completely dissolve the polystyrene, so you were left with the guck. Packing chips are also made from polystyrene, but as they are thicker than the coffee cup, they can take longer to soften.

STRANGE . . . BUT TRUE!

There is an extremely rare medical condition called *hypertrichosis* that has only been seen in about 50 people in the world. How would you know if you had this condition? Well, your face and other parts of your body would be covered with a thick layer of hair. We aren't talking about a long beard or a few stray hairs on the sides of your face. Imagine if all the hair on your head was growing on your face or body. People have nicknamed this condition "Werewolf Syndrome."

7. ZOMBIE FOOD

Zombies like to eat rotting flesh. In this next activity you can make some "rotting" food of your own!

You Will Need:

- an adult helper
- ¾ cup (180 mL) flavored drink or juice
- a small saucepan
- a stove
- a package of unflavored gelatin
- two identical loaf pans
- a spoon
- wide plastic drinking straws
- a bag of rice or another heavy object

What to Do

1. Have an adult bring the flavored drink or juice to a boil in the saucepan.
2. Place the gelatin in one of the loaf pans and have an adult pour the boiling liquid, a little bit at a time, into the pan. Use the spoon to stir until the gelatin has dissolved.
3. Let the liquid cool to room temperature.
4. Lay the straws flat into the liquid, making sure the liquid covers the straws.
5. Place the second loaf pan (with the flat side down) into the pan with the liquid, and place the bag of rice or other heavy object into the pan. This will weigh down the straws so they don't float above the liquid.
6. Place the pans in the fridge and allow the gelatin to set. After several hours, remove the pans from the fridge and separate the straws. Squeeze out the "snakes" by running your fingers down the straws.

I ATE WHAT? WHAT HAPPENED?

Gelatin contains a protein (yes! another polymer) made from animal skin and bones. Like guar gum, gelatin is a thickening agent. If you hadn't added the gelatin to your juice, it would have remained liquid and would not have set.

You can find gelatin in many things that you eat, including gummy candy, marshmallows, and pudding.

STRANGE . . . BUT TRUE!

Scientists in Sweden have discovered a type of "zombie worm" that lives off the bones of dead whales. They have given the creature the name *Osedax mucofloris*, which loosely translates as "bone-eating snot flower." The name is a pretty accurate description, as these tiny worms look like mucus-covered flowers poking out from the whale bones.

8. LEVITATING SPIRITS

What goes up must come down . . . or must it? Can an object just hang in midair? Is it possible for a spirit to levitate? Let's see. . . .

You Will Need:

- a straight pin
- a piece of plastic twine made up of shiny plastic fibers (found in hardware stores) about 4 inches (10 cm) long, or a thin opaque plastic bag
- a pair of scissors
- wool fabric
- 2 feet (60 cm) PVC plumbing pipe that is around ½ inch (1 cm) in diameter

What to Do

1. Use the straight pin to tease apart the fibers at one end of the piece of plastic twine. Leave about 1 inch (2.5 cm) of the twine still connected together. If you can't find twine, you can cut a 4-inch (10 cm) by ½-inch (1 cm) piece of plastic bag and use scissors to make a thin fringe by cutting 3 inches (7.5 cm) into one end several times. This is your "spirit."
2. Fold the fabric in half and hold the connected end of the spirit in one hand. Pull the fibers through the wool fabric. Do this several times.
3. Rub the PVC pipe with the wool fabric several times.
4. Toss the spirit into the air and move the PVC pipe underneath.

GOSH! WHAT HAPPENED?

When you rubbed the spirit with the wool cloth, you gave the plastic a negative charge (see "Ghost Legs," pages 44–45). The PVC pipe was also given a negative charge when it was rubbed with the wool. When electrical charges are the same in two objects they tend to push each other away, or repel each other. The spirit you made is very light so the repulsion from the like charges was strong enough to hold it suspended over the pipe.

STRANGE . . . BUT TRUE!

If you love visiting your living relatives, how about spending time with your dead ones? On November 2, people who live in Mexico and parts of Latin America celebrate the Day of the Dead, or *El Dia de los Muertos*. Those who have lost loved ones get together and celebrate the lives of the dearly departed. Family members bring special foods and gifts to the graves.

9. ALIEN BARF

Do you have a terrible fear of vomit? That's called emetophobia. Vomit smells terrible, but it's your body's way of removing foods you probably shouldn't have eaten. If living creatures exist on other planets, they probably also have to vomit. Have you ever wondered what alien vomit would look like?

You Will Need:
- food coloring
- a small plastic or glass jar
- ½ cup (120 mL) white glue
- a wooden stir stick
- 2 tablespoons (30 mL) liquid laundry starch
- a dinner plate
- bits of plastic toys, plastic soda bottle caps, etc.
- a sealable plastic bag

What to Do
1. Place several drops of your favorite shade of food coloring in the small jar and add the white glue. Use the stir stick to mix.
2. Slowly add the liquid starch a drop at a time to the colorful glue goo, and continue stirring with the wooden stick until the goo looks like vomit.
3. Remove the goo from the jar, place it on a dinner plate, and mix in various plastic items that you think an alien would eat. The goo will keep in the sealable plastic bag for several days. When you're finished, use the bag to throw it away.

GAG ME OUT! WHAT HAPPENED?

Your alien vomit was actually another type of polymer. You made it using the PVA in the glue and the **starch**. This polymer is stringy and the water from the liquid starch gives it a vomitlike appearance. If you have ever thrown up just after eating, you know that your barf can contain food that hasn't yet been digested, and the plastic parts you added might just be food for an alien.

STRANGE ... BUT TRUE!

You eat polymers, but not the plastic type. The proteins, fats, and starches that you eat are polymers. You break them into smaller parts when you eat them.

If you aren't allergic to wheat, try this: Ask an adult for an unsalted soda cracker. Slowly chew on the cracker. At first the cracker seems starchy, but the longer you chew on it, the sweeter it begins to taste. The chemicals in your saliva begin to break down the starch in the cracker. As this happens, the starch in the cracker changes into sugar, which is why the cracker seems sweeter. Starch is a natural polymer made from sugar.

10. MESSAGES FROM BEYOND

Is your bathroom haunted? Can spirits from another world leave you messages on your mirror? Is it science or a spectral image that appears?

You Will Need:
- a bathroom with a mirror
- lots of steam from a hot bath or shower

What to Do
1. After someone has taken a hot shower or bath, see if the mirror in the bathroom is fogged up. If it is, use your finger to write a message like "Boo!" or draw a ghostly picture.
2. Allow the fog to dry on the mirror, and do not wipe the mirror with a towel. Don't tell anyone else you have created this message.
3. The next time the bathroom mirror is steamed up, your family is in for a surprise.

HELLLP! WHAT HAPPENED?

When you wrote your message on the mirror, your finger left behind small amounts of oils. Those oils made it more difficult for water droplets to later form on the surface you touched. The mist formed on the rest of the mirror, allowing your family member to read the message.

11. RUBBER BONES

Chances are you have never heard the word *caoutchouc*. It is a very fancy word for "rubber," which comes from the sap of a rubber tree. Getting this word on a spelling bee may be scary, but what chills will it bring to your spine in this experiment? Let's see. . . .

You Will Need:
- an adult helper
- a bone from a cooked chicken
- white vinegar
- a jar with a lid

WARNING: Never handle chicken bones from a raw or uncooked chicken. Wash your hands with soap and water after touching chicken.

What to Do

1. Ask an adult to clean the meat, white cartilage, and any veins, skin, or stringy stuff from a chicken bone. The bone must be completely clean before you begin.
2. Put the bone in the jar and add enough vinegar to cover it. Put the lid on the jar and leave it on the counter for about a week.
3. Take the bone out of the vinegar and rinse it in water. Pour the vinegar down the drain. Hold the bone on either end and try to bend it. If the bone doesn't bend, put it back in the jar and cover it with fresh vinegar. Leave it there for another week and try this step again.

COOL! WHAT HAPPENED?

You may have read that milk, or rather, the **calcium** in milk, is good for your bones. Vinegar, however, is not so good for bones. The chemical in bones that makes them hard and strong is calcium phosphate. When an **acid** like the one in vinegar or the one in soda, is in contact with calcium phosphate, a chemical reaction occurs. This reaction makes the calcium in the bones dissolve in the vinegar. Once the calcium is no longer in the bones, the bones become soft.

STRANGE . . . BUT TRUE!

If you ever find yourself in Prague, in the Czech Republic, take the time to visit the Sedlec Ossuary. The bones of over 40,000 people are arranged around the church and form elaborate art pieces, including chandeliers, bells, coats of arms, crowns, and other decorations. The grounds of the church were considered sacred, and many people wanted to be buried there. In the early 1500s the bubonic plague killed 30,000 people, and their bodies provided the building materials for adorning this unusual church.

12. THINGS THAT GLOW IN THE DARK

If your path crosses that of a black cat at night, the only things you might see are its creepy, glowing yellow eyes. Cats' eyes have a special membrane at the back of their eyeballs that reflects any light in the area, so they appear to glow. Other things can absorb and reflect light to glow in the dark, as you will see. . . .

You Will Need:

- a glass of tonic water
- a black light (available at hardware stores)
- a pair of plastic or latex gloves
- petroleum jelly
- paper
- paper money

What to Do

1. Place the glass of tonic water in front of your black light and turn on the light. What do you see? This works best if the room is dark and only the black light is turned on.
2. Put on a pair of plastic or latex gloves. Dip your finger in petroleum jelly and write a message on a piece of paper. Hold the paper up to the black light and see what happens.
3. Put more petroleum jelly on the gloves and hold your hands near the black light. Oohhh . . . spooky!
4. Look for hidden messages or shapes on money using the black light. Do you see any?

WHOA! WHAT HAPPENED?

Black light isn't actually black. It is a little bit of purple light and a lot of a type of light called **ultraviolet**. We can't see ultraviolet light, but we can see the effect it has on certain materials. The items that glowed absorbed some of the ultraviolet light and gave off visible light. We call these types of items **fluorescent**.

STRANGE . . . BUT TRUE!

Scientists at the University of California have discovered that when they unroll sticky tape, they get bursts of X-radiation. These X-rays are the same type of radiation a dentist uses to check your teeth for cavities. When the tape is unrolled, the tape becomes negatively charged and the glue becomes positively charged. Scientists believe that the difference in the charges is enough to cause X-rays to be released.

13. BUBBLING ALIEN BLOOD

Science fiction movies often portray creatures from outer space as having green, yellow, or blue blood that bubbles when exposed to Earth's atmosphere. See if you can fool your friends into believing you are from another planet.

You Will Need:

- 1 tablespoon (15 mL) baking soda
- 1 tablespoon (15 mL) corn syrup
- green, yellow, or blue food coloring
- a small jar
- a wooden stir stick
- an eyedropper
- ¼ cup (60 mL) white vinegar

What to Do

1. Place the baking soda, corn syrup, and a few drops of food coloring in the jar, and use the stir stick to mix the ingredients until a smooth paste is formed.
2. This next part is messy, so make sure you are wearing old clothes and perhaps consider doing this outdoors or while standing in the bathtub. Do not do this next step over a carpeted area. Use the wooden stir stick to apply this paste to your hand, arm, or leg. Do not put this on any part of your body that has a cut, and do not put it on your head or face.
3. Fill the eyedropper with white vinegar and drip the vinegar onto the "blood." Stand back!

WOW! WHAT HAPPENED?

The bubbles were caused by a chemical reaction. The reaction produced carbon dioxide gas, which formed the bubbles you saw. The corn syrup and food coloring just made this look more realistic!

STRANGE . . . BUT TRUE!

If you were to suddenly find yourself in space without a spacesuit, you would die very quickly. But your blood wouldn't boil, as some people believe. Space is cold, mostly dark, and has no **atmosphere** — no air to breathe and no air pressure. You wouldn't be able to breathe and would most likely pass out within around 15 seconds.

14. BOUNCING EYES

In a scary movie, you might see an alien creature carrying its eyeballs and holding them high to see what's around. Pretty creepy . . . Want to try making rubbery alien eyes of your own?

You Will Need:
- a hard-boiled egg
- an uncooked egg
- two containers
- white vinegar

What to Do

1. Place each egg in a container and completely cover both with vinegar. Put the containers on a flat surface and let them sit overnight. The next day, pour out the old vinegar and replace it with fresh vinegar.
2. Put the containers back on the counter and leave them there for at least two weeks.
3. When the shells have dissolved, remove the eggs from the vinegar and rinse them under cold water.
4. Gently drop the eggs on a flat plate (do not try this over a carpeted area). Do they bounce? If the eggs didn't bounce, clean up the mess. Can you feel the "pupils" of the egg "eyeballs"?
5. Pour the vinegar down the drain. Do not eat the eggs, and make sure you wash your hands after you have touched the eggs.

COOL! WHAT HAPPENED?

The vinegar reacted with a chemical in the eggshells called **calcium carbonate**. When this happened, the eggs' shells dissolved. When the shells dissolved, the raw eggs began to swell up and they became larger. This was caused by water in the vinegar moving into the egg through osmosis (see "Shrunken Heads," pages 6–7). The boiled egg became more rubbery and may have even bounced a bit when you dropped it. The raw egg also became more rubbery, but it may have broken apart when dropped. The addition of vinegar acts to make the proteins in eggs clump together. This process is called denaturation. Proteins **denature** when they are heated, as in cooking, or when they are mixed with acids, like the one in vinegar.

15. VAMPIRE BITES

Despite the popularity of all things vampire, they do not exist. However, there are vampire bats, whose main source of food is blood. And there are people who are **photosensitive**, who cannot go out in the sun and must live their lives in the shade. Here's a way to look like a vampire.

You Will Need:

- 1 tablespoon (15 mL) citric acid (available with the canning supplies in grocery stores)
- 1 tablespoon (15 mL) baking soda
- ¾ cup (180 mL) icing sugar
- red food coloring
- a clean food container
- a spoon or wooden stir stick

What to Do

1. Place the citric acid, baking soda, icing sugar, and a few drops of food coloring in the clean food container and use the spoon or stir stick to mix the ingredients together. Now, stand in front of a mirror or a friend for the next part.
2. Work up a mouthful of spit, and then place a small amount of the powder on your tongue. Open your mouth and stick out your tongue. Do not swallow the foam — let it flow out of your mouth.

YUCK! WHAT HAPPENED?

When the powders were dry, nothing happened. As liquid — your saliva — dissolved the powders, a chemical reaction between the baking soda and the citric acid began in your mouth. The reaction produced carbon dioxide gas, which was the foamy bubbles. The sugar wasn't part of the chemical reaction, but without it the mixture would have really tasted terrible and the bubbles would have been thinner.

Remember: Never taste real blood. It's very dangerous and you could get extremely sick.

STRANGE . . . BUT TRUE!

There is a condition called porphyria that is a possible source of the vampire myths. People with this condition can be photosensitive: Their skin can blister when they are in the sun. They also often have receding gums due to light exposure, which can make their teeth look longer, like vampire fangs. Even their urine is different: It can be a reddish color, which may explain why vampires are said to eat or drink something different . . . like human blood.

16. SHOCKING!

A door creaks open and the mad scientist's lair is revealed. Come into the lab and see what scary things you can find. They will shock you!

You Will Need:

- an adult helper
- a short, thick candle
- a match or lighter
- a disposable metal pie plate
- a thumbtack (optional)
- a Styrofoam plate or an old vinyl record
- a piece of wool or silk fabric

What to Do

1. Have an adult light the candle and drip wax into the center of the pie plate. When there is a large blob, blow out the candle and press the unmelted, flat end firmly into the liquid wax. If you want to, you can also stick a thumbtack through from the bottom of the plate into the base of the candle.
2. Rub the surface of the Styrofoam plate or old record with a piece of wool or silk.
3. Holding the pie plate by the candle handle, place it on top of the charged Styrofoam plate or old record.
4. In a darkened room or closet, bring your finger near the pie plate, and then touch it.

OUCH! WHAT HAPPENED?

When you rubbed the record or plate with the fabric, you transferred extra **electrons** to that object, giving it a negative charge (see "Ghost Lights," pages 48–49). This charge pushed some of the electrons in the pie plate away to the edge of the pie plate. These electrons jumped across into your finger, giving you a shock and giving off a bit of light as they moved through the air.

STRANGE . . . BUT TRUE!

When a person suffers a heart attack, emergency response teams frequently use two "paddles" that carry a large electric charge. When these paddles are placed on a person's chest they transfer that electric charge to the person's body, which can cause the heart to start beating again.

17. EXPLODING STOMACH

Have you ever eaten so much that it felt like your stomach was going to explode? That can't really happen, can it? You don't need to eat anything for this activity, but it'll give you an idea of what's going on in your digestive system.

You Will Need:
- an Alka-Seltzer tablet or about 1 tablespoon (15 mL) baking soda
- a plate
- a spoon
- a balloon
- a funnel
- ¼ cup (60 mL) white vinegar

What to Do

1. If using an Alka-Seltzer tablet, place it on the plate and use the back of the spoon to crush the tablet into a fine powder.
2. Stretch the mouth of the balloon over the small opening of the funnel. Carefully pour the vinegar into the funnel a bit at a time, allowing it to go into the balloon.
3. Spoon the Alka-Seltzer powder or baking soda into the funnel and shake it gently to make sure all the powder also goes into the balloon. Remove the funnel, and tie a knot in the neck of the balloon.
4. Put down the balloon and stand back (this could get messy).

FIZZ . . . WHAT HAPPENED?

A chemical reaction occurred between the acid in the vinegar and a chemical in the powder. The chemical in the powder is called sodium hydrogen carbonate, or sodium bicarbonate. When the reaction was finished, the balloon was larger because it contained extra carbon dioxide gas.

STRANGE . . . BUT TRUE!

No, if you eat certain candies and drink soda, a chemical reaction in your stomach will not cause your stomach to explode. This is an **urban myth**. However, it was reported by a number of credible news sources that in 2005 a 13-foot (4 m) Burmese python's stomach exploded when it tried to eat a 6-foot (1.8 m) alligator in the Florida Everglades. According to eyewitness reports, and confirmed by photographs, the alligator's remains were found sticking out of the dead python's burst midsection — the snake's head was nowhere to be found.

18. GOBLIN LAMP

What type of lamp do you think goblins and ghouls should have? We think that lava lamps, with swirls of colored liquids, are the spookiest. Here is a lava lamp you can make for yourself the next time you feel a little ghoulish!

You Will Need:

- a funnel
- a clean, clear, small plastic soda bottle with a lid, and the label removed
- vegetable oil
- water
- food coloring
- glitter, confetti, or small beads (optional)
- four Alka-Seltzer tablets
- a flashlight (optional)

What to Do

1. Use the funnel to fill the soda bottle about three-quarters full with vegetable oil. Then add water until the bottle is almost filled. Add food coloring, a few drops at a time, until the mixture is fairly dark. If you like, you can also add some glitter, confetti, or small beads.
2. Break each Alka-Seltzer tablet in half. Break each piece in half and then in half again, until you have made eight pieces from each tablet.
3. Drop the pieces of Alka-Seltzer into the bottle one at a time, waiting until the bubbling stops each time before adding another piece.
4. When you have used all of the Alka-Seltzer, put the lid back on the soda bottle and seal it tightly. Place the bottle on its side and gently lift each end of the bottle so that the liquid inside sloshes back and forth. You can even illuminate the bottle by shining a flashlight underneath it.

WOW! WHAT HAPPENED?

The food coloring you added colored the water, but not the oil. This is because the molecules that make up the water and the food coloring are attracted to one another more than they are attracted to the oil molecules. When you added the Alka-Seltzer pieces, they fell through the oil layer, and when they hit the water they reacted to give off bubbles of carbon dioxide gas. The bubbles disturbed the oil and water as they moved up and out of the bottle, stirring the mixture and making it look like a lava lamp. You also disturbed the oil and water when you sloshed the liquids together in the sealed bottle, which gave a "wave" effect.

19. GHOST LEGS

Ghosts roaming the earth have to wear something, don't they? How else would we know they exist? Apparitions in movies either have a cloudlike whitish appearance or are invisible; you just see what they wear or move around in. Let's see if a ghost is the only nonliving thing that can fill out some clothes.

You Will Need:

- a piece of plastic wrap
- a nylon stocking (not a pair of pantyhose)

What to Do

1. Crumple the piece of plastic wrap and hold it in one hand.
2. Use your other hand to hold the toe of the nylon stocking against a wall.
3. Stroke the stocking from the toe to the opening using the crumpled plastic wrap.
4. After two minutes of stroking, remove the stocking from the wall and hold it in the air. Watch what happens.
5. Bring the plastic wrap near the stocking, and watch what happens now.

SHRIEK! WHAT HAPPENED?

You created an electric charge called **static electricity**. When you rubbed the plastic on the nylon, some of the electrons moved from the nylon to the plastic. Electrons have a negative charge, so the plastic became negatively charged and the stocking became positively charged. When charges are the same, they push each other away, so the sides of the stocking pushed away from each other. Different charges are attracted to each other, so the stocking moved toward the wrap. When the wrap and the stocking were close enough together, the electrons jumped back onto the stocking with a crackling sound.

STRANGE . . . BUT TRUE!

Lightning is an enormous version of the tiny electrical discharge you created with the nylon and plastic wrap. Negatively charged particles hurtling through the sky create heat and light, and rapid superheated air around the lightning causes thunder. There are about 100 lightning strikes on Earth every second. So, whenever you hear the rumble of thunder, remember to seek shelter indoors if you can. If you can't get indoors, keep your feet close together and crouch down low to the ground with only your feet touching the earth until the lightning moves away. And don't use a phone or get caught in a pool.

20. HATCHING SNAKE EGGS

Have you heard about the girl who couldn't wash her hair because she had a tight braid? One day her friend was looking at her hair and found tiny spiders crawling in the rows. The friend took out the braid to find that spiders had laid eggs all over her head. Okay, it isn't actually a true story; it's really another urban legend. But here are some "eggs" you can safely hatch.

You Will Need:

- an adult helper
- a very large and thick paper clip
- a pair of wire cutters (optional)
- a rubber band
- a round toothpick (optional)
- an envelope

What to Do

1. Unfold the paper clip to create a large U shape. One end of the paper clip will be longer than the other.
2. Have an adult trim the longer end of the paper clip to make both ends the same size. This can be done using wire cutters or by bending the piece back and forth to break the wire. If you do not have a toothpick, do not throw away the broken piece of wire.
3. Place a rubber band across the U-shaped end close to the top, or open end, of the wire. The rubber band should be just wide enough not to bend the wire, and not loose enough to slip off the wire.
4. Put the toothpick or small piece of wire that was broken off the paper clip between the sides of the rubber band and twist or wind the piece until the rubber band won't turn any longer. Make sure the toothpick or wire piece is short enough to be able to rotate between the rubber band and the bottom of the wire U. The toothpick or wire may need to be trimmed to fit.
5. The next part may take some practice. Hold the wound toothpick or wire steady so that it doesn't unravel, and slide it into the envelope. Use one hand to hold down the envelope while you remove your hand from the toothpick.

6. Close the flap of the envelope, but do not seal it.
7. Hand the envelope to an unsuspecting adult or friend and tell them you have collected some snake eggs from the garden. Watch what happens when they open the envelope. You can even decorate the envelope with a picture of a snake or a warning.

EEEEEEK! WHAT HAPPENED?

When the envelope was opened, the rubber band unraveled, causing the wire or toothpick to hit the sides of the envelope. Because the person who was holding the envelope was told it contained the eggs of a creature, the sound the wire created made the person think the eggs were hatching.

STRANGE . . . BUT TRUE!

Bird eggs have a special shape. For example, if you gently push a chicken egg on a counter, the egg will roll in a circle. This is because bird eggs have an oval shape that prevents them from rolling out of the nest. Unlike bird eggs, snake eggs are oblong. The mother snake lies on top of these eggs, and the shells are like tough leather, and not like the fragile shells of chicken eggs. Now for the gross part. Some kinds of snake eggs need to be kept moist. The best way to do this is for the mother snake to urinate on the eggs. Ew!

21. GHOST LIGHTS

A light tube lights up, and it isn't even in a light fixture! It must be magic or the work of ghosts because everybody knows you need to use electricity to light up a lightbulb. Or do you?

You Will Need:
- an adult helper
- a balloon
- a clean, dry fluorescent light tube

WARNING: Light tubes are made of thin glass and can be easily broken! Do not handle the bulb yourself. It must be handled with care by an adult only.

What to Do
1. On a dry day, blow up the balloon and tie the neck of the balloon closed.
2. With an adult gently holding the light tube, take the balloon and the light tube into a dark room or closet. Hold the balloon in one hand while an adult holds one end of the light tube. Let the other end of the light tube rest on the floor.
3. Rub the balloon back and forth across your hair several times.
4. Hold the balloon close to the tube and move it along the tube without the balloon and tube touching.

46

YIKES! WHAT HAPPENED?

Even though it wasn't connected to a fixture, the tube was connected to electricity: static electricity. Rubbing the balloon on your hair moved electrons from your hair onto the balloon. This gave the balloon a static charge. When the balloon moved near the tube, the static charge made electrons inside the tube move. Fluorescent tubes contain, and are coated with, materials that cause them to glow when even a small electric charge is applied, so the tube lit up.

STRANGE . . . BUT TRUE!

There are professional "ghost hunters" who claim to be able to scientifically prove a place is haunted. They use **infrared cameras**, digital voice recorders, and sensitive instruments that measure changes in temperature. They also take readings of differences in **electromagnetic fields**, which the hunters believe will show if a "spirit" is present in a home. Despite using scientific equipment, these hunters have yet to prove the existence of spirits.

22. SPOOKY WRITING

Wouldn't it be neat to read a secret message? Maybe even one left behind by a scary goblin or ghost? Here's a ghostly experiment that has a scientific basis.

You Will Need:

- 1 tablespoon (15 mL) baking soda
- a small glass
- ¼ cup (60 mL) warm water
- a toothpick
- paper
- a paintbrush
- grape juice

What to Do

1. Put the baking soda into the glass. Add the warm water to dissolve the baking soda.
2. Stir the solution with the toothpick and then use the toothpick to write a secret message on a piece of paper. Allow the paper to dry.
3. Dip your paintbrush into the grape juice and paint over the baking-soda message.

OOOOH, AAAAH! What Happened?

Grape juice contains a type of chemical called an anthocyanin that acts like an **acid-base indicator**. That means the chemical turns a different color when it is placed in an acid chemical than it does when it is placed in a **base** chemical. The baking soda is a base chemical, and it changes the purple grape juice to blue. If you did this same experiment using an acid like vinegar or citric acid, the writing would turn a more reddish hue.

STRANGE . . . BUT TRUE!

Lobsters can change color just like grape juice. When lobsters are alive, they can be blue or a brownish orange, but when they are cooked, they all turn red. Lobster shells have red **pigment** — the substance that gives them color — but they also have proteins that denature when they are cooked . . . so just like leaves that turn red in fall when the green pigment degrades, lobster shells turn red because that is what is left after their proteins lose their shape.

23 GHOST FOOD

Sometimes people see images of famous people's faces in food. The next time you read about a piece of toast that had an image of Elvis on it, here's one explanation of how it got there.

You Will Need:

- lemons
- a saucer or cup
- a paintbrush
- a piece of white bread
- a toaster

What to Do

1. Squeeze some fresh lemon juice onto a saucer or into a cup.
2. Use the paintbrush and the lemon juice to paint a message or a picture onto the bread. Allow the lemon juice on the bread to dry.
3. Place the bread in the toaster and lightly warm the bread. Do not toast the bread. Pop the bread from the toaster while the bread is still white.

HEY! WHAT HAPPENED?

When the lemon juice was warmed, it turned darker. Although lemon juice tastes very sour, it contains sugars. These sugars **caramelized** and turned brown when the bread was heated. Bread also contains sugars, but the sugars from the lemon juice were more concentrated in the area of your secret message, so the message became visible when the bread was lightly toasted.

24. BLACKOUT

Are you afraid of the dark? It can hide just about anything. Here's a fun way to hide something behind the blackness.

You Will Need:
- white paper
- a black **indelible**, or permanent, marker
- a black washable marker
- a bucket or bowl
- water

What to Do
1. Write a message on a piece of white paper using the black indelible marker. Something short like "Boo!" is good for your first try. Let the markings dry completely.
2. Scribble over the message using a black washable marker until you can no longer read the original message. Let the markings dry completely.
3. Now, give the message to your friend. Have him or her dip the message into a bucket or bowl full of water and swish it back and forth until the message is readable.

NEAT! WHAT HAPPENED?
Washable markers use water as a **solvent**, so most of the black pigment can be removed using water. Indelible markers use other chemicals as their solvents, so their pigments stay behind on the paper. Water takes a bit longer to evaporate than the solvents used in indelible markers, so you may have noticed that the washable marker took longer to dry.

STRANGE . . . BUT TRUE!

Are you terrified of snakes? Do spiders make you scream? How do you feel about flying? If you are afraid of something, there's probably a name for the thing you dread. The word *phobia* means "fear." Here are some common phobias:

Arachnophobia: fear of spiders
Arithmophobia: fear of numbers
Aviophobia: fear of flying in planes
Brontophobia: fear of thunder and thunderstorms
Claustrophobia: fear of closed spaces
Mysophobia (also known as germphobia)**:** fear of germs
Necrophobia: fear of dead things
Ophidiophobia: fear of snakes
Paraskavedekatriaphobia: fear of Friday the 13th
Triskaidekaphobia: fear of the number 13

And if you have this fear, skip the next word:

Hippopotomonstrosesquippedaliophobia: fear of long words

GLOSSARY

Acid – a sour substance that forms water and a salt when mixed with a base

Acid-base indicator – any chemical that turns a different color when more acid is added or more base is added

Albumin – a type of protein found in egg white

Amplify – to increase

Atmosphere – all of the gases surrounding Earth

Base – a bitter substance that forms water and a salt when mixed with an acid

Calcium – a chemical element found in shells, bone, and teeth

Calcium carbonate – a salt found in chalk and limestone

Caramelize – what happens when carbohydrates are heated to a certain temperature and change color

Denature – to break apart or alter the structure of molecules, usually by heating or exposing them to chemicals

Electromagnetic field – an energy field surrounding electrical devices

Electron – a tiny negatively charged particle that is part of all atoms

Evaporate – to change in state from a liquid to a gas

Fluorescent – giving off light when it is illuminated by light of a different color

Indelible – difficult to erase or remove

Infrared camera – a camera that will take photographs of objects that give off heat or infrared radiation

Molecule – a tiny particle that consists of two or more atoms joined together

Osmosis – the movement of water from a weak solution toward a more concentrated solution

Photosensitive – having a reaction to light

Pigment – a substance that gives color to other materials

Polymer – a chemical with large molecules made up of smaller molecules linked together

Polyphenol – a bitter or sour-tasting chemical found in plants

Polystyrene – a type of plastic commonly used for packaging materials

Protein – a polymer made up of amino acids and found in all living things.

Solvent – a liquid or gas that can dissolve other substances

Starch – a polymer found in plants that is made up of sugars

Static electricity – a buildup of electric charge on an object

Ultraviolet – light that is at the very edge of the blue side of the light spectrum

Urban myth – a widely circulated modern story that is untrue